Red Rocket™ Readers

Let's Go Surfing

written by Pam Holden

Teacher Talk

"Are you a good swimmer? You could go to a sandy beach to learn to surf. The waves get bigger and then they break and turn white. A helper can show you how to pick a wave that is coming straight in. You will learn how to ride towards the beach. Next you will learn how to stand up on your surfboard and balance as you ride. You will have lots of practice and fun!"

Key Words

best better learn left must right someone whit

Teaching Plan

- Use Teacher Talk to stimulate discussion about surfing.
- Develop research skills based on this topic.
- Use the Table of Contents to find specific information.
- Refer to the Glossary to clarify basic concepts.
- Use initial letter plus visual clues to read unknown words.
- Locate compound words: **surfboard** **someone**
- Notice silent letters: **right** **know** **learn** **white** **straight**
- Discuss new vocabulary: **breaking** **goofy-footed** **balance**
- Understand use of exclamation marks and question marks.
- Promote drama, writing or art as creative follow-up activities.

Word Count = 283

First published in 2016 by Red Rocket Readers, an imprint of Flying Start Books Ltd.
Big book edition first published 2017.
13/45 Karepiro Drive, Auckland 0932, New Zealand.

story © Pam Holden
ISBN 978-1-776542-39-0
Printed in New Zealand
All photographs supplied by iStock Photo

Let's Go Surfing

Contents **Page**

written by Pam Holden

Are you a good swimmer?
If you go to the beach you can learn to ride the waves.
Surfing is fun.

You must have someone to help you.

You will need a small surfboard.
It will have a leg rope.

You can lie or stand on it.
There are fins under the board.

First you must learn all about the waves.
Watch the way the waves get big.
Then they break into white surf and
come in to the beach.

Look for waves that are coming straight.
Watch how other surfers catch rides.

Go into the water with your helper. Put your board in the water and push it out. Jump over the white waves. Find a wave that has just broken.

Turn around and get on your board.
Get a push from your helper. Go!
Lie flat and enjoy the ride!

Go back out to where the waves are breaking. Take as many rides as you can.

Soon you will know how to paddle as a wave comes to you.

Next you will learn how to stand up. Your helper will show you the right way. You will push up with your arms.

Find out which way to stand. If you put your right foot in front that is called goofy-footed. Some surfers like to put their left foot in front. Which way is best for you?

Get to know all about
the waves.
Jump in front of a wave
that is coming to you.
Stand up and put out
your arms to balance.
Sometimes you will fall
into the water!

Go surfing as often as you can. You will get better and better until you are a good surfer. Have fun!

balance	do not fall over
enjoy	have fun
fin	thin piece to help through water
goofy-footed	right foot in front
paddle	use arms to move through water
straight	not going left or right
surf	white foam on breaking waves

Fluency Level 1
Non-Fiction Set C

GUIDED READING	R/R INTERVENTION	LEXILE MEASURE
J	15	500L

F&P Text Level Gradient™
Officially Leveled by Fountas & Pinnell

CERTIFIED LEXILE® PARTNER

Red Rocket™ Readers

Engineered by Flying Start Books

redrocketreaders.com

ISBN 978-1-776542-39-0

9 781776 542390